Native Americans

Southeast Indians

Mir Tamim Ansary

Heinemann Library
Des Plaines, Illinois

© 2000 Reed Educational & Professional Publishing
Published by Heinemann Library,
an imprint of Reed Educational & Professional Publishing,
Chicago, IL

Customer Service: 888-454-2279

Designed by Depke Design

Printed in Hong Kong

04 03 02
10 9 8 7 6 5 4 3

Library of Congress Cataloging-in-Publication Data
Ansary, Mir Tamim
    Southeast Indians / Mir Tamim Ansary
        p. cm. – (Native Americans)
    Includes bibliographical references (p.   ) and index.
    Summary: Introduces the history, dwellings, artwork, religious
beliefs, clothing, food, and other elements of life of the Native
American tribes of the Southeast.
        ISBN 1-57572-924-5
        1. Indians of North America—Southern States Juvenile literature.
    [1. Indians of North America—Southern States.] I. Title.
    II. Series: Ansary, Mir Tamim. Native Americans.
    E78.S65A656 1999
    975.00497—dc21   99-13516
                                                      CIP

Acknowledgments
The Publishers would like to thank the following for permission to reproduce photographs:
Cover: Ben Klaffke
Dr. E.R. Degginger, p. 4; Stock Montage, Inc./Theodore de Bry, p. 6; Thomas Gilcrease Institute, Tulsa,
Oklahoma/George Catlin, p. 8; Corbis-Bettmann, pp. 9, 27; Ben Klaffke, pp. 10, 20, 21; New York Public Library,
p. 11; Smithsonian Institution, p. 12; Cherokee Historical Association, p. 13; National Geographic Society/Victor
Boswell, p. 14; North Wind Pictures, pp. 15, 17; St. Louis Art Museum/Charles F. Wimar, p. 16;
Morton/Milon/SPL/Photo researchers, p. 18; The Granger Collection, pp. 22, 25, 30; Archives and Manuscripts
Division of the Oklahoma Historical Society/Dedrick, p. 26; Lawrence Migdale, p. 28; Micco Aircraft Company,
p. 29; The Library of Congress, p. 24.

Every effort has been made to contact copyright holders of any material reproduced in this book.
Any omissions will be rectified in subsequent printings if notice is given to the publisher.

Our special thanks to Lana Grant, Native American MLS, for her help
in the preparation of this book.

Note to the Reader Some words are shown in bold, **like this.** You can find
out what they mean by looking in the glossary.

Contents

The Southeast Region

Long ago, a thick forest stretched from the Mississippi River to the Atlantic Ocean. Some of this forest still stands. This area is warm and wet. Rain falls in every season. Summers are hot, and the air is so moist it feels heavy.

This area is called the Southeast. In some places, there are big, rolling hills. In other places, the land is flat. Lazy rivers run through the whole region. In the far south, swamps are common. The soil is rich, however, and plants grow easily.

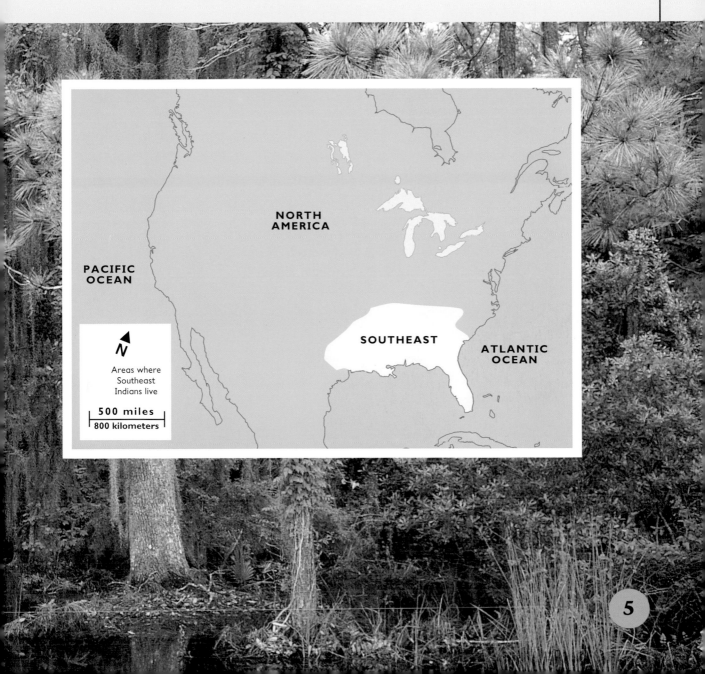

NORTH
AMERICA

PACIFIC
OCEAN

SOUTHEAST

ATLANTIC
OCEAN

N

Areas where
Southeast
Indians live

500 miles
800 kilometers

Early People of the Southeast

The first settlers entered this region from the north. They came about four thousand years ago. They made huge mounds as graves for their leaders. Then around **A.D.** 700, new groups started moving north from Mexico. These people built mounds to hold up **temples.** And around these temples grew big cities.

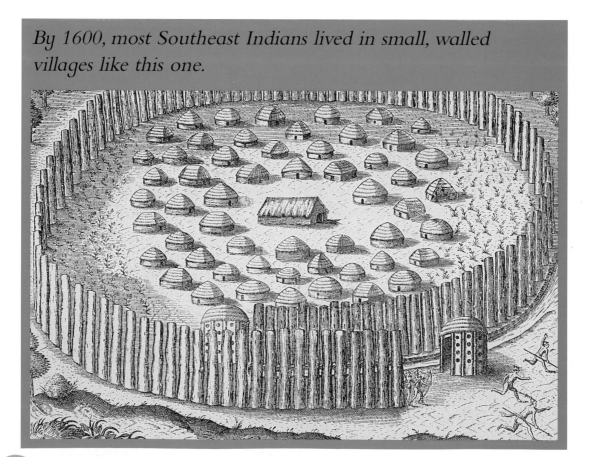

By 1600, most Southeast Indians lived in small, walled villages like this one.

After 1200, however, these cities emptied out. No one knows why. By 1500, all the tribes of this region were living in smaller villages. Each tribe had a group of villages. The Natchez, for example, had nine. The Cherokees had 60. Each village had about one hundred families.

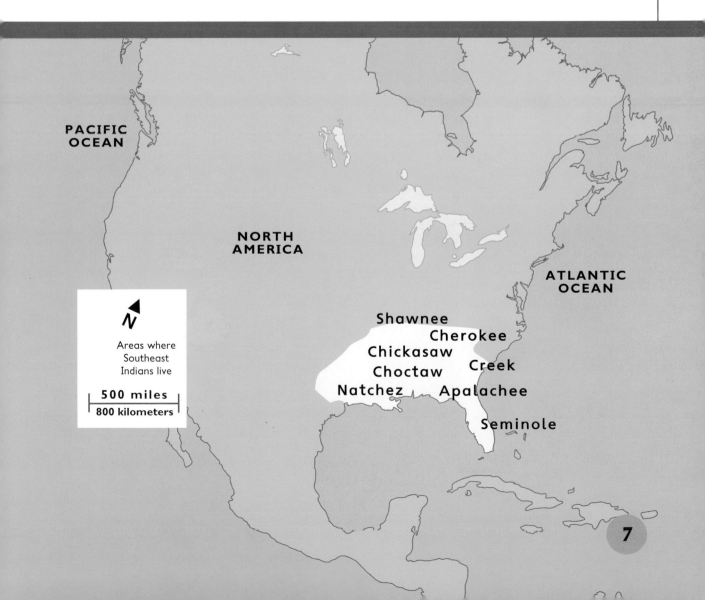

PACIFIC
OCEAN

NORTH
AMERICA

ATLANTIC
OCEAN

N

Areas where
Southeast
Indians live

500 miles
800 kilometers

Shawnee
Cherokee
Chickasaw
Choctaw   Creek
Natchez   Apalachee
Seminole

Farmers and Hunters

The villagers of the Southeast were good farmers. Corn was their main **crop.** But they also grew squash, pumpkins, and tobacco. Whole villages worked together in spring and summer. Men plowed. Women tended crops. Children scared away animals that might eat the crops. Then in the fall, each family harvested its own crops.

Whole villages worked together to farm and gather wild foods.

Southeastern Indian men hunted white-tailed deer and other game.

The Native Americans of the Southeast did not just farm. They were hunters, too. Men used bows and arrows to shoot wild turkeys, bears, and deer. They were expert **trackers**. A hunter sometimes put a deerskin over his body. This way he could sneak right into a herd of deer.

Clothing and Decoration

Deer provided not only meat but clothing. Women would scrape and pound a **hide** till it was soft as cotton. From this leather, they made shoes called moccasins. They made dresses and jackets for the winter. They made **leggings** to protect their skin from thorns in the woods.

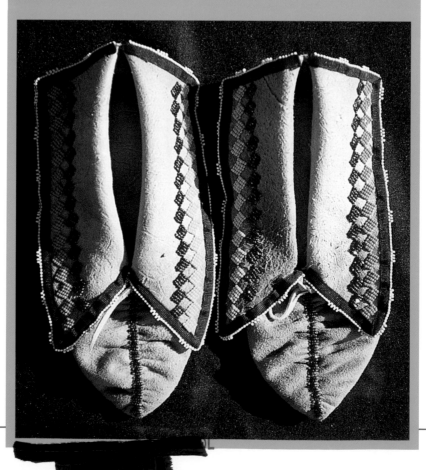

These Creek moccasins are made of deerskin and decorated with beads.

Both men and women in the Southeast used feathers as decoration.

In the hot months, children wore nothing at all. And grown-ups wore very little. But people liked to "dress up" with decorations. Men had fancy hair styles such as **topknots.** Both men and women wore tattoos and body paint. They pierced their ears and noses to wear **ornaments.**

Homes and Villages

Native Americans of the Southeast built roomy homes. They started with a frame of bent poles. Over this, they plastered mud and straw. Summer houses often had no walls, just a roof. Most villages were along a river. And most had a wall of logs around them for protection.

This Seminole house provided shade from the hot Florida sun.

Sometimes a river or stream ran right through an Indian village in the Southeast.

Every Southeast village had a big, central open area. Here, people got together for games, meetings, and feasts. The chief's house was here. So was a big building called "the great house." This was used for meetings, parties, and other events. More than one hundred people could fit inside it.

Government and Family

Southeast Indian tribes were divided into **classes**. People in the lowest class had little power. Those in the **noble** class received great respect. Nobles made the big decisions. At the very top was the chief, who was special. The Natchez, in fact, treated their chief like a god.

The Natchez carried their chief so his feet would never touch the ground

Children in a Southeast family belonged to their mother's clan.
Their father was of a different clan

Villages were also divided into **clans.** People of
the same clan could not marry each other. When
a man got married, he moved in with his wife.
But he was like a visitor in her house. The children
belonged to the mother's clan. Her brothers
supported her and helped raise her children.

Going to War

War between tribes was common in the Southeast. This is why most villages had walls. Battles, however, were small. Men went out in groups of about 30. They walked single file in each other's footprints. That way, a **tracker** could not tell how many were in the group. Warriors fought hand to hand with clubs.

By the 1800s, Indian warriors like these Seminoles were using guns.

This man's tattoos show that he has fought bravely in many wars.

Courage was greatly honored. Men who proved their bravery in war could rise to a higher **class.** Boys went to war as teenagers. They could not get a tattoo until they had done a brave deed in war. Each new deed earned them another tattoo. The greatest warriors had the most tattoos.

The Spirit World

In the Southeast, people believed in many nature spirits. They saw the sun as the most powerful god. Fire was another face of this god. Most villages kept a **sacred** fire burning all year round. The Creeks put this fire out each fall and started a new one. These customs are still practiced today.

Indians believed that the earth and sky were filled with living spirits.

The Creeks **mourned** a death for a year or more. Yet their belief in life after death was already strong. Like other Southeast tribes, they believed that brave people went to a world of endless woods and fine hunting. The Milky Way was seen as a path to this wonderful place.

Festivals and Games

In late summer, many tribes celebrated the Green Corn Festival. This was a New Year festival—a time to start over. All crimes except murder were forgiven. Old clothes were burned. Whole villages bathed together. Men drank a black liquid that made them throw up. This was thought to make them pure inside.

The Green Corn Festival was the highlight of the Indian year.

Stickball and other games were popular at a Green Corn Festival.

Then the fun began. People put on new clothes. They sang and danced. They feasted on new "green" corn. Young men played ball games such as lacrosse. In this sport, each team might have hundreds of players. The Cherokee called this rough sport "the little brother of war."

The Europeans Arrive

In 1540, a Spaniard named Hernan de Soto marched through the Southeast. Other Europeans soon followed. The English, French, and Spanish fought each other for this land. The Indians took sides—but they often picked the losing side. In the American Revolution, they sided with the British.

In 1776, the United States was founded. After that, white settlers swarmed through the Southeast. The native people tried to push them back. But the settlers had better weapons. Also, European diseases had already killed or weakened many native people. So the white settlers won.

This painting shows Hernan De Soto at the Mississippi River in 1541.

After the Wars

By the early 1800s, many Cherokees, Choctaws, Creeks, Seminoles, and Chickasaws had given up their old ways. They were known as the Five Civilized Tribes. They were living and dressing like Europeans. Many had become Christians. A man named Sequoyah invented an alphabet for the Cherokee language. The Cherokee started publishing a newspaper.

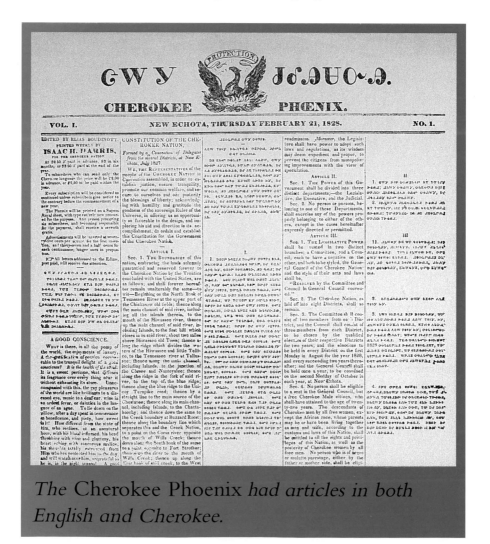

The Cherokee Phoenix had articles in both English and Cherokee.

About 18,000 Cherokees walked "The Trail of Tears" to Oklahoma.

But white settlers still wanted Indian land. A law was passed that said the government could force Indians to move. In 1838, the Cherokees were forced to walk more than 1,000 miles (1,609 kilometers) west. Many died along the way. The Cherokee remember that winter march as "The Trail of Tears."

Hard Changes

The Seminoles moved into the swamps of Florida. They fought the U.S. Army from 1835 to 1842. They were never beaten. Most Southeast Indians, however, ended up in what is now Oklahoma. This land was bare and dry, very different from the Southeast. Each tribe was given a **reservation,** a land set aside for Native Americans.

Much of Oklahoma is flat grassland, like this area in Dewey County.

In the 1800s, much Indian land was given away or sold cheaply to whites.

In the late 1800s, Oklahoma reservations were broken up. Each Indian family was supposed to get 160 acres of land. Any land left over was sold to whites or given away. The Cherokee struggled to survive as small farmers. Some started businesses. In World War One, many joined the U.S. Army. But many Cherokee remained poor.

Southeast Tribes Today

Today, the Cherokees are the biggest Native American tribe. They are U.S. citizens, but they also have their own **tribal** government. In 1985, Wilma Mankiller was elected chief of the Cherokee Nation. Under this strong leader, the Cherokee built new strength. Today, Cherokees can be found in all walks of life.

Wilma Mankiller was a strong Cherokee chief.

The Seminole tribe's Micco Airplane Company built this plane.

Some Native Americans still live in the Southeast. The Seminoles of Florida run many successful businesses. For example, the Micco Airplane Company makes small airplanes. Seminole Chief Jim Billie is a pilot himself. With strong new leaders, Native Americans of the Southeast are making a new place for themselves in America.

Famous Southeast Indians

Will Rogers (Cherokee: 1879–1935) Rogers started out as a rodeo cowboy in Oklahoma. He became one of America's best-loved entertainers. In books and radio shows, he poked friendly fun at important people. Later, he acted in more than 60 movies. He died in an airplane crash.

Osceola (Seminole: 1800–1838) Osceola was a Seminole chief in 1832. That year the United States ordered the Seminoles to move to Oklahoma. Osceola refused. He led a war against the U. S. Army in the Florida swamps. He was captured in 1837 and died in prison the next year.

Wilma Mankiller (Cherokee: 1945–) Wilma Mankiller was chief of the Cherokee nation from 1985 to 1995. In that time, the tribe grew by one hundred thousand members. Mankiller worked to give Cherokees better homes, schools, and jobs.

Glossary

A.D. means *anno Domini* in the Latin language and shows that a date comes after the birth of Jesus Christ

clan group of related families

class rank of a person or group in a society where people are not equal

crop farm product, usually a plant grown for food

hide skin of an animal

leggings clothes that cover just the legs

mourn show sadness about a death by actions

noble person or family who is considered more important because of his or her family

ornament body decoration such as jewelry

reservation land set aside for Native Americans

sacred that which is treated with great respect for religious reasons

spirits beings who have life and power but cannot be seen

temple building used for religious worship

topknot one long clump of hair at the top of a shaved head

tracker person who can find people or animals by following footprints and other clues

tribal having to do with a tribe

More Books to Read

Lepthien, Emilie U. *The Choctaw.* Danbury, Conn.: Children's Press, 1992.

Lund, Bill. *The Seminole Indians.* Danbury, Conn.: Children's Press, 1997.

Roop, Peter. *If You Lived with the Cherokee.* New York: Scholastic Incorporated, 1998.

Index